AMANDA ST

The Tween Mother's
TOOL BOOK

Raising Strong Daughters

The Tween Mother's Tool Book: Raising Strong Daughters

Author: Amanda Stokes

Copyright © 2020

ISBN: 9780648345831

www.raisingstrongdaughters.com.au

Subjects: Parenting | Family Relationships

Book production: Bev Ryan, www.smartwomenpublish.com

A catalogue record for this book is available from the National Library of Australia

Disclaimer

The material in this publication is of the nature of general comment only, and does not represent professional advice. It is not intended to provide specific guidance for particular circumstances and it should not be relied on as the basis of any decision to take action or not take action on any matter which it covers. Readers should obtain professional advice where appropriate, before making any such decision. To the maximum extent permitted by law, the author and publisher disclaim all responsibility and liability to any person, arising directly or indirectly from any person taking or not taking action based on the information in this publication.

Contents

Acknowledgements

To my husband Simon I would like to say thank you. I am so grateful for your support and for the belief you have shown in me as I have brought this book to life. To my children, thank you for choosing me to be your mum. We may not always get it right, but we are a living example of working daily to be our best selves. I love you for the lessons you teach me and the love that you share.

I also want to give special thanks to the talented tweens whose art pieces appear amongst the pages of this book. You are so talented, and you captured so beautifully the thoughts and intentions of this book. I am truly honoured.

I Love This Book

As soon as Amanda reached out to me to share her book, I was all in. I'm a solo mum, and while my daughter and I have spent most of the past five years traveling together and navigating challenges and tricky situations, the upcoming tween years had me scared. How would I help her through without losing my patience, hurting her feelings or not giving her the right guidance and support?

As I started reading *The Tween Mother's Tool Book* my panic subsided, and I was equally relieved and energised. I felt like I had a friend right by my side to help me navigate these complex, emotional years we were entering, and I soaked up each tip and worksheet, feeling more confident with every page I turned.

Amanda gently offers simple, practical ways for us mums to support our daughters through their tween years – through the sunny days and the storms. Working through the Tool Book has given me greater confidence that my daughter and I will grow and bond as we approach these years together.

Making agreements with our daughters about how we respect and support each other sets a valuable foundation, and the tools in Amanda's book give both mums and daughters the awareness and guidance to tackle the challenges we know are on the way – like body confidence, moods, friendships and instilling self-belief.

No matter how different we may be, there's no doubt we all want to help our daughters become confident, strong and brave young women. Through activities and guided journaling, Amanda helps us understand ourselves, our triggers and how our upbringing and our past can impact our own parenting. This insight is so important to developing the best relationship we can with our daughters.

My daughter and I are already benefiting from Amanda's guidance, and I am confident we will emerge from these years still holding hands. I am sure you and your daughter will too.

Evie Farrell
Solo parent, author, and explorer
www.mumpacktravel.com
@mumpacktravel

Preface

My own story of growing up is a happy one. I was brought up by a single mum who only married because in 1975 it wasn't the done thing to have a child out of wedlock. By the time I was thirteen months old, my parents were divorced and my relationship with my father had all but ended.

I was an only child, which meant that my mum and I became a team, and an incredibly close one at that. Fortunately for me, I had no one to share her with, and her attention on me was undivided. I say fortunately because I spent most of my childhood being asked if I wished I had siblings, or if I wished I had a dad. I used to hate those questions, and so I took a positive approach from very early on, being grateful for what I had instead of pining for what was missing. It is my experiences that have made me who I am, and to this day I wouldn't wish it any other way.

It wasn't until I grew up and had my own children that I really understood the sacrifices my mum must have made in her life to give me all I had. She wasn't perfect, but whose mother is?

In 2002, as a fresh-eyed graduate teacher, I took on my first twenty-eight kids; they became my children. I remember like it was yesterday the love I had for that class. Each and every one of those children brought their own unique energy into the group each morning. It was always my goal to embrace each child for who they were, quite apart from their test scores and the dots that appeared on their data charts.

At that point I loved everything about teaching, but my greatest interest was in learning how to help each child become amazing from the inside. I wanted them all to know that they were special, that their differences were worth celebrating, and that they needed to be proud of who and what they were.

I started reading parenting books, and the one that still stands out to me today as the best was *How to Talk So Kids Will Listen & Listen So Kids Will Talk*, by Adele Faber and Elaine Mazlish. The book blew my mind. In it were practical and simple methods of helping kids feel heard, and I put these into practice on a daily basis in my classroom. I created a space where my students felt seen and heard, and I worked to give them strategies to overcome hardships.

One of my favourite memories is of the box I kept near the classroom door, along with paper and a pen. I told the class that anything they wanted me to know about but didn't feel comfortable saying to me out loud could go in the box. I promised anonymity, and then used the issues and concerns the children had as opportunities, mainly by brainstorming strategies and ideas to provide support during classroom circle time.

On some level, my aim was always to normalise life for my students. I think many of us feel alone and different as children, and often we don't learn until later in life that everyone has similar fears and worries. It's not until we starting talking about those fears and worries that we realise it.

I ran a lunchtime club for students, where I would start by raising a friendship-issue problem based on something I'd heard students talking about. I would then invite the children in the club to come up with alternative ways of handling the problem. Their ideas would often blow me away.

That was eighteen years ago.

Before becoming a mother myself, I had a feeling deep in my heart that I would be incredible at it, that I'd be a natural. After all, I was patient with the kids in my class. I was empathetic. But I only ever saw my students between 9 am and 3.15 pm from Monday to Friday.

To me, parenting was easy. I was judgemental towards my students' parents. I found it too easy to cast blame without knowing the inner workings of the individual families. Quite simply, I didn't understand what parenting actually meant.

And then in 2009 I became a mother for the first time. In my mind, I was still certain that I would find being a mum easy. In my mind, I was still sure I would be a natural.

I still remember the moment the nurse left us with our crying baby. I looked over at my husband, with the unspoken words between us: *What on earth are we going to do now?*

Our son, our precious newborn, screamed for the first three months of his life. He would only fall asleep on me. I was beyond exhausted, and felt so far in over my head. At the time I had quite a few close friends who also had babies, but they all seemed to have 'good' ones, babies who settled easily and slept through the night. I felt like I had a broken one.

But time passed and we got through it.

At the end of 2010 our first daughter was born. I knew what to expect the second time around, but, being honest, I have to say that most of the early stages of her life are a blur.

Fast forward to mid 2013, and the final piece of our family puzzle arrived: a second daughter. Our family of five was closed for business. Well, my uterus was, anyway.

I can't say I loved my children's younger years. I certainly didn't love having small babies, with the nappies and sleeplessness. During the terrible twos and the threenage years, I longed to be able to reason with my kids, to talk to them instead of bearing witness to 40-minute tantrums because I'd given them the wrong colour plate.

People always say that you shouldn't wish your life away—my grandmother would say it to me often—but different stages of life can bring out the best and the worst in us and I'm very glad those days are behind me.

My children are now eleven, nine and seven, and I feel capable of dealing with them at this stage of their lives. After all, I've been training for this moment for most of my adult, professional life.

This age in our children's lives is when we get to make the biggest impact on who they will become. These are the tween years, those years where they are not yet teenagers but they're not little kids anymore.

These are monumentally important years. These are the years where we as parents can help our children lay the groundwork for their lives.

We can help them develop the skills to navigate their relationships and regulate their emotions—which can be huge—and work with them on becoming the very best version of themselves they can be, in a world that will often try to knock them down.

Introduction

This book has always lived in me. It's a compilation of all the things I wish I'd known when I was growing up, and contains useful, practical thoughts and ideas. You will find out how to help keep important lines of communication open as your daughters head towards their teen years, taking them further away from you and your role as mum, life guide and significant other.

It is my passion to help provide our daughters with the tools they need to enter a world that isn't always kind, with warmth in their hearts and a deep understanding that they are always worthy, even when those around them may not see it.

The years leading up to your daughter becoming a teenager are some of the most important and challenging years of her life. As she transitions from your compliant, loving little girl into a young woman aware of her own wants and needs, she will push the boundaries—and your buttons—as she works to find her place in the world, no doubt trying on many hats as she navigates the path to becoming the person she wants to be when she grows up.

If you think back to when you were her age, you will likely be able to recall a certain amount of struggle. There may have been friendships that didn't last the course, arguments where you tried to assert yourself, and rebellion as you fought to gain a degree of autonomy from your parents.

And then you became a mother, and maybe you've forgotten what it was like to be your daughter's age.

How strange is it that the only precursor to becoming a parent is having been a child.

If you could go back in time, what do you wish your own mum had understood about you? What do you wish she had done with you to create a relationship where you felt less misunderstood throughout those tween/teen years? What would have made your journey from child to young adult easier?

You can't turn back the clock on your own childhood experiences, but my hope is that *The Tween Mother's Tool Book* will provide opportunities for you to become the parent you yourself needed during those incredibly important in-between years.

One of my beautiful girlfriends, who had attended one of my mother-and-daughter workshops, shared with me that she and her Miss Nine had used some of my take-away activities during isolation through the pandemic. The activities had helped lift the mood of both mum and daughter, and inspired some great discussions between them. Hearing her words filled my heart with so much joy. In that moment, I knew that I wanted to create a guide for mums with daughters, something that could be easily accessed and referred to, and readily available to support them both as they travel through the challenges of the tween years.

Think of this book as your coaching manual. It's the supportive hand on your shoulder when you feel lost and out of options. It's your wise, non-judgemental friend who has great ideas for improving the connection between you and your daughter. It will help you keep the communication channels open with your tween. Think of it as your parenting toolkit, the light that will illuminate what can often be a rocky road as you navigate the tween years.

I hope the information within this book helps you navigate some of those trickier areas, reminds you that you're not alone, and encourages you to believe that you're doing a great job of mothering, even when you may not feel that you're getting it right.

We are so much stronger together.

As a mum, with this powerful tool book in your hand you are empowered. You are holding the keys to a more connected, open, supportive, and engaged relationship with your daughter, and I could not be happier.

There is no right or wrong way to use the book. It definitely doesn't have to be read from start to finish, although that would be a great way to familiarise yourself with the content. Whether you're experiencing poor behaviour, looking for more effective communication strategies, or struggling to find ways of helping your daughter feel better about herself, you will find guidance and support within these pages.

And if you're looking for more, you could consider joining The Mother's Hub Club at Raising Strong Daughters [www.raisingstrong-daughters.com.au] a place for parenting support and mentoring that represents real life, in real time. Benefits include weekly live Q&A sessions to cover whatever is going on in your world, so please take a look if you think this is something you would benefit from.

I'm excited about the connection I know this book will help you create with your daughter as she goes through her tween years.

When we know better, we can be better.

Please note that you can also download printable copies of all activities in this book in pdf format from www.raisingstrongdaughters.com.au.

Chloe C, Age 8

1

CREATING A FAMILY ESSENTIAL AGREEMENT

*a*t the start of every school year, your daughter probably participates in creating an essential agreement; an agreement arrived at and agreed upon by all the members of her learning community. It's a way of deciding communally what the requirements are for a class to run effectively, and to ensure that everyone has input into making the classroom a place where they all feel safe and included.

I believe that families need an essential agreement too. Your family most likely already has one, even if it hasn't actually been written down. Your agreement includes the things you allow and the things you don't, the standards of behaviour you accept and don't accept, and your expectations.

As your daughter enters her tween years, it's an important time to set up a shared family agreement, one that is negotiated, discussed, and agreed upon by all, and displayed in a shared area as a reminder.

Choose a night where you know you will all come together as a family, with no distractions or demands on your time, and come up with your family's essential agreement. Everyone in the family should contribute; everyone has a voice, and everything is up for discussion.

Once you've come up with your top five or six things, have everyone sign off on it and then display it in a common area where it can be referred back to readily.

Some questions to help you come up with your family's essential agreement:

- What does a happy home look like?
- How can we maintain a happy family environment?
- What can we do to make each other feel heard?
- How can we help each other feel good about ourselves?
- What behaviours support a positive home?
- How can we become more responsible for our actions?
- What would be reasonable consequences for breaking our agreement?

Don't forget to include a discussion on technology, if this is an issue in your home. A great starting question would be: *How long do you think is a fair and reasonable amount of time to use devices?*

When we involve our children in important discussions like this, they feel a sense of ownership, and are often more compliant when it comes to the consequences of overstepping because they have been part of the decision-making process.

Being part of the discussion doesn't mean your daughter is in charge of the final decisions—some things will be non-negotiable—but allowing her to be included in the conversation is an important step towards the development of her growing independence. When things go pear shaped, as they undoubtedly will, and poor behaviour rears its ugly head, you will have something concrete to refer back to and remind her of.

A shared agreement is a powerful one. Your family's essential agreement could be built around the format on the following pages.

Our Family's Essential Agreement

In our family these are our top five values:

1. _____

2. _____

3. _____

4. _____

5. _____

In our family everyone deserves to be treated

_____

_____

_____

_____

We can show each other we care by

_____

_____

_____

_____

_____

The consequences of not following this agreement are

_____

_____

_____

_____

_____

Signed:

_____

_____

_____

_____

Tamara B, Age 12

2

REFLECTIONS ON CHILDHOOD

When we become parents, we often forget what it was like to be the child. I'd go so far as to say that sometimes we act like we skipped childhood altogether, and were born disciplined and correct, without ever experiencing the sense of fun that children possess so naturally.

Often the parent we become is based on the experiences we had as a child. If your parents were overly strict and authoritative, you might attempt to make up for what you experienced by being very relaxed, perhaps too relaxed. If your parents lacked boundaries and you were allowed to run free, you may parent in the same manner because you know no other way.

This is an interesting concept to reflect on.

You might look back at certain times in your childhood and wish your parents had been more like your friends' parents, or that they had understood you better. Maybe they never let you do anything and so you had to sneak around. Perhaps you wish they'd trusted you more, or were fairer in their actions and decisions.

This is the time to think back. This is your chance to understand why your parents were the way they were, and perhaps tweak your own parenting to be a little more considerate of the needs of a tween daughter. This doesn't mean you should become a pushover and give her everything she wants. That's not a good approach for anyone. But it can only be a positive move to look closely at the role you play in your relationship with your daughter and ask yourself some difficult questions:

- Do I talk down to her sometimes?
- Am I overly authoritative?
- Am I always giving in to her because I don't want her to be upset?
- Do I need to be right all the time?
- Am I an I-told-you-so mum?

Reflecting on how you mother can be difficult. It can be hard to admit that you aren't doing it right, but do you know what's worse than not getting it right? Never realising that there was a better way.

I'd like to let you in on a little secret that I want you to remember: no one gets it right all the time. There is no such thing as a perfect parent. No one really has it all together, not all the time, anyway. The purpose of this book is to help you recognise when you could be doing things a little better. There's no blame and no guilt, just reflection and learning. There are no qualifications for raising children; we all do the best we can, and when we know better, we can be better.

The thing I love is that during this process, you will be role-modelling something powerful to your daughter. Even when you think she's not noticing or paying attention, believe me, she is. She will be taking in everything you do, even when it's not obvious to you.

In the activity on the next page, choose as many options as apply. The purpose of this task is to reflect on how you were parented when you were growing up.

My Childhood

When I was growing up my parents were:

Relaxed	Tired	Angry	Kind
Balanced	Fair	Unfair	Hardworking

When I was growing up, I felt:

Empowered	Trapped	Happy
Frustrated	Confident	Sad

I wish my parents had given me more:

Of their time	Freedom	Money
Experiences	Structure	Attention

My parents made me feel that:

I was special	I was a failure	I was trouble	I was the best
I was in the way	I was smart	I was funny	I was loved

My favourite childhood memory is

_____

_____

_____

_____

_____

One thing I would have changed about the way my parents raised me is

_____

_____

_____

_____

_____

3

LOOKING BACK AT YOUR YOUNGER SELF

*I*f you could go back in time to when you were your daughter's age, what would you say to yourself? As a grown woman, what do you wish your younger self had known?

As a young girl, I remember being quite shy in new situations. I also remember feeling forgettable. If I saw someone I knew when I was away from home, I avoided eye contact at all costs. I was never the main girl in my group of friends. I was never the funniest or the prettiest or the one that others were drawn to.

When I think back, perhaps that's where my feelings of not being special or memorable began. I remember feeling a little invisible. I didn't attend the outside school groups that my friends attended. I didn't have brothers and sisters. I didn't feel connected the way those around me appeared to be. I can still recall feeling unseen.

I was, however, very lucky. I belonged to a family where I felt very loved, where I felt seen; within my family I knew I was important.

Although I didn't have an unhappy childhood, there were definitely aspects of those early years that I wish I could change. Then again, without the journey I've taken, I wouldn't be who or where I am today. I like to think of myself as an example of 'grow through what you go through', one of my favourite sayings of all time.

If you did have the opportunity to go back in time, even if only for a few minutes, what would you say to your younger self if she stood before you right now? Keep in mind that your younger self lives on in you, buried deep within the many life experiences that have shaped you until this point.

If I had such an opportunity, I would remind my younger self that even when she felt like she wasn't important, she was. I would encourage her to walk with her head held high, to make eye contact, to smile at the people she knew, knowing that they *would* remember her. I would tell her to be friendlier and to not shy away; in fact, I would say the exact words I now find myself saying to my tween.

I would also tell my younger self that my body was amazing, and that even though my mum battled with *her* body, I didn't have to battle with mine. I would teach my younger self the many ways there are of being smart.

At school, I remember feeling like my teachers didn't think I was clever. I was terrible at maths, I didn't do my homework, and as a consequence I always sensed my teachers' frustration and disappointment in me. When I became a teacher myself, I vowed to become the teacher I'd needed when I was growing up, a teacher who saw a child as a whole person, a teacher who understood that there are many different ways of being smart.

I would tell my younger self that I was, in fact, *very* smart; that I was creative, that I was witty, that I was observant, and that I was so much more than the scores I got on my times tables tests.

What would you say to your younger self? The time is now. Using the next page as inspiration, let it out. Express all the things your inner child should have heard. Do some repair work; make peace with your past. Forgive yourself for the things you didn't know before you knew them. The future starts now.

Letter to My Younger Self

_____

_____

_____

_____

_____

_____

_____

_____

_____

_____

_____

_____

_____

_____

_____

_____

_____

_____

_____

_____

_____

4

BECOMING A
ROLE MODEL

From now on, I want you to think of yourself as the coach of your daughter's tween team. Your job is to help with her skills development, show her the important plays in life, and teach her how to navigate challenges as they arise. Be there at the end of a game, or after a hard day at school. Encourage her to reflect on what has happened that day, and help her work out what she can learn from her experiences in order to deal with things better next time.

As a coach, your role is more supportive than authoritative. It allows for mistakes, it focuses on growth and learning; it's about building up rather than knocking down. The coach has the player's back, but the player is the one who makes the final moves. The coach empowers; the player delivers. The coach's job is to model appropriate ways.

Let your daughter witness you admitting your mistakes, particularly where she's also involved. When you fail, own that failure with your head held high. Learn from your errors, be better than you were yesterday; let your daughter see you striving to be the best version of yourself that you can be.

There is so much power in this. Tell your daughter that you believe in her. Remind her that she's not defined by her mistakes in life, but rather how she picks herself up again. When you do this, you are leading by example time and time again.

You are her greatest role model during these tween years, when you are still her queen, the person she looks up to and aspires to be like. This won't continue into her teen years—in all likelihood you will suddenly become her greatest source of embarrassment—so take it while it lasts.

Be the best role model you can be for her, because she will be watching and she will be listening. Be someone who builds other women up.

As women, we sometimes fall into the trap of believing we are in competition with one another. It's as though we get the idea in our heads that there's a pot of goodness somewhere out there, and if someone takes from it there will be less for us. This leads to jealousy and envy, which creeps in and ruins how we feel about one another.

By celebrating other women, you can show your daughter that there's enough goodness to go around. You can show her that you're aware that another woman's success or beauty doesn't take away from your own. As a role model, you can demonstrate that the only person you're in competition with in this life is yourself.

What a gift it is to be able to help your daughter understand that she doesn't need to compare herself to others, and that another girl getting an award doesn't mean that she is any less worthy; all it means is that the other girl deserves to be celebrated.

Your job is to teach these things to your daughter by being a role model for her, because she may not learn these valuable lessons on her own.

Fill this jar with all the things you would choose to celebrate about someone else.

Celebrating Others

Take some time now to write a letter to your daughter. Open up to her about your hopes, your fears and your joys. Give your daughter an opportunity to know you as a girl who was once her age. This allows her a precious opportunity to see you as who you once were, and allows you an opportunity to reflect and remember being her age.

Letter to My Daughter

Dear _____

When I was your age I dreamed of being

_____

_____

My saddest moment was when

_____

_____

_____

_____

_____

_____

My happiest memory is of

_____

_____

_____

_____

_____

I'll never forget the time my mum and I

I always wished

I'm so grateful that

Love forever
Mum xx

5

CREATING OPPORTUNITIES TO LISTEN

This is an important chapter, because knowing ourselves and understanding why we react and respond the way we do matters. We can probably all think of a few adults we know who haven't mastered this skill yet; people who blame others for everything, lack self-awareness, and never believe anything is their fault. Those who lack self-awareness also fail to take responsibility for their actions because they never see the part they play in events.

We all play a role in life, and sometimes we play many roles. We are never just one thing. We can be shy and yet outgoing, depending on whom we are with. We can be stubborn with our families, but easy-going with our friends. All of this is perfectly normal as long as we're aware of it.

Do this activity with your daughter. Sit together and ask her to choose which qualities she sees in herself, and you do the same for yourself. Do you see each other differently than you thought?

Choose which of these qualities relate to you

- ☐ Outgoing/shy
- ☐ Listener/talker
- ☐ Grateful/ungrateful
- ☐ Glass half full/glass half empty
- ☐ A risk taker/the safe lane
- ☐ Need to be right/okay with being wrong
- ☐ Jealous of others/happy for others
- ☐ Understood/misunderstood
- ☐ Responsible/carefree
- ☐ Popular/unpopular
- ☐ Powerful/weak
- ☐ Curious/uninterested
- ☐ Followed/follower
- ☐ Reactor/thinker
- ☐ Confident/lack confidence
- ☐ Excited for the future/afraid of the future

A valuable way of helping your daughter is to ask her questions about when she feels either powerful or weak. A few sample questions:

- What does it mean to have power in a friendship?
- Do you feel powerful? Why/why not?
- How do you think someone can make themselves more powerful?
- Who do you know who is weak? What do you think of them?

These questions should trigger conversations that give you powerful opportunities to listen to what your daughter has to say. Perhaps you'll hear her talk about her desire to be more popular or accepted. Maybe she will even share her struggle, and her desire to become more assertive towards those who wield power.

Let her talk and make sure you *really* listen. If it feels appropriate, share an experience about yourself, but if you judge that it's not the right time, save that conversation for another day. When the time is right, you could say something like: *Do you remember what we talked about the other day? It made me think about something that happened when I was your age.* Then share your story.

Be aware of taking over the conversation without realising it. Guard against directing a conversation away from your daughter to yourself. Judge whether the best thing to do is to listen or to share. Your daughter can learn so much from you. Be open, but pick your moments.

Some things you can talk about to help normalise your daughter's own experiences:

- Tell her what you were like when you were her age.
- Relate your experience of being popular or unpopular, and how that affected you.
- Be open about whether you were grateful as a child.
- Tell her what you had, and what you wished for.
- Share with her the things you were worried about.

This conversation doesn't have to take place all in one go. After all, there may be a lot to unpack. Do what feels right for you and your daughter at the time. If it feels like too much, revisit these questions another time.

Mikayla D, Age 10

6

DEALING WITH LIFE'S STRUGGLES

I n this chapter we focus on the ways in which we accept our individual struggles. I remember once reading about butterflies and their final stage of transformation. When it's time for a butterfly to leave its cocoon, it must go through an enormous struggle as it fights its way out of the cocoon's tiny opening with its shrivelled wings. If someone who meant well were to help the butterfly by creating a larger opening, the butterfly would not be able to fly. It's the struggle that makes flight possible, by pushing the fluid out of the butterfly's body and into its wings. Without that struggle, the butterfly never becomes what it is meant to be.

I love this story for so many reasons.

As parents we often want to protect our children from struggle. We want them to have an easier life than we did. We think we're helping them, but it is their struggles that give them strength.

The following activity allows for a discussion between you and your daughter around strengths and weaknesses. Its purpose is to normalise life's struggles and to teach the importance of self-awareness as your daughter transitions to becoming a butterfly.

THE TWEEN MOTHER'S TOOL BOOK

Strengths and Weaknesses

What are your three greatest strengths?

1. _____

2. _____

3. _____

What are your two favourite things to do?

1. _____

2. _____

What are three things you've succeeded at recently?

1. _____

2. _____

3. _____

Why were you successful?

_____

_____

_____

_____

How do you feel when you struggle with things?

_____

_____

_____

_____

Do you think struggling with things makes you stronger? Why/why not?

_____

_____

What are two of your least favourite things to do?

1. _____

2. _____

Why did you choose those two particular things?

_____

_____

What two things seem harder for you than for other kids your age?

1. _____

2. _____

How do you think those things can become easier for you?

_____

_____

What can I do to support you when things are hard?

_____

_____

_____

Everyone struggles; even people you don't think struggle, struggle. It's normal; it's part of being human. It's okay to admit that there are things you find hard.

Now share a few of your struggles with one another, free of judgement.

Take some time to reflect. What are the things you struggle with? Are you kind to yourself or do you put yourself under a lot of pressure? Remember that you are the role model. It's normal to struggle but it's important for you to reflect on how you deal with your struggles.

Things I Struggle With (for Mums)

Things I Struggle With (for Daughters)

_____

_____

_____

_____

_____

_____

_____

_____

_____

_____

_____

_____

_____

_____

_____

_____

_____

_____

_____

THE TWEEN MOTHER'S TOOL BOOK

7

THE POWER OF
THE PAUSE

Teach your daughter the power of the pause. When our children are in their tweens their impulse control is usually not great, but you can teach them to think about the impact their words and actions have on others by encouraging reflection. First, take an honest look at yourself. How do you react when you're angry? Are you an exploder? Do you struggle to regulate your emotions in the moment? If you realise that you're modelling ineffective behaviour, that's okay as long as you're honest with yourself and work towards creating more effective strategies.

As a young person I would say the first thing that came into my head. My best friend and I would get into arguments and say hurtful things to one another in anger. We never meant the things we said, it was just the way we fought, a little like sisters who hate each other one minute and love each other the next. This communication style became our normal.

When I began dating my husband, however, I was forced to create a new way. My husband does not say hurtful things out of anger. He pauses, he processes, and he thinks before he speaks. I'm so grateful that I was able to change my ways because it's allowed me to be a much more positive role model for my children than I would have been if I was still reactive. I now have effective strategies to use to calm myself down, and I can often be found in the kitchen counting, sometimes to ten, sometimes to a hundred. These days you will never hear me saying hurtful things in anger—not outside of my head, anyway.

The pause is such an important strategy to use when we're angry because it buys us time. It gives us time to respond. It allows us to recalibrate, cool down and compose ourselves. It prevents us from saying things we will regret.

Again, this is something that needs to be taught. I can't count the number of times I've heard my own children threaten to block their friends online when they're angry with them, or have had kids at school tell me that someone said they were never going to play with them again.

The things we say out of anger are not the things we mean, so teaching the pause is an important skill when it comes to considering how much of what we say we actually mean, and how much belongs to anger.

8

IMPLEMENTING THE PAUSE

If you have a tween daughter like mine, you will no doubt find yourself dealing with emotional outbursts and reactions that take her from zero to a hundred faster than a speeding bullet. As a parent, it can be frustrating to watch these heightened responses to events that range from a request from a sibling to move her feet, to an argument over whose turn it is to hold the remote.

Post outburst, I used to ask my daughter what she thought she could do differently in terms of her reaction the next time she found herself in a similar situation. She would always answer that she didn't know, saying it wasn't her fault and the others were to blame for making her so angry.

We began talking about self-control, and the idea of someone making you do something and taking away your power. We discussed how our bodies send us signals, but that we have to recognise those signals in order to be able to respond to them. In our discussions we covered a lot of ground: we are in control of our actions; nobody can make us do something without our permission; our choices are ours to make.

Over the years I have spent a lot of time working with my tween daughter after her meltdowns, and have come up with techniques and strategies she can use when she begins to feel her heart rate increase and blood pressure rise. I explained that without this awareness, she would repeat the same behaviour over and over.

There is no quick fix, but with time and patience we can all make progress towards new and more appropriate ways of coping.

If you have a daughter who struggles to regulate her emotions, she should find the following activity helpful.

My Calm-Down Plan

When I find myself getting angry, I can:

- Leave the situation
- Count to twenty in my head
- Ask for some space
- Remind myself that it isn't as bad as it feels
- Go to my room and yell into my pillow
- Write in my journal
- Do a meditation
- Listen to some calming music
- Practise the pause
- Go for a run
- Get some fresh air
- Focus on slowing my breathing

More items to add to my list:

_____

_____

_____

_____

_____

_____

_____

Georgia L, Age 11

9

COPING WITH YOUR DAUGHTER'S MOODS

Try not to take your daughter's moods or bad behaviour personally. I repeat, do not take it personally. Believe it or not, your tween will often be unaware of her tone, and she may not hear the things she says the way you do. I know; it seems hard to believe.

A helpful way to encourage your tween daughter to really hear herself is to say something like: *When you talk to me in that way it makes it hard for me to listen to you. Can you please try saying that another way?* This will give her a chance to try again.

If this approach fails, you could say: *I understand you're frustrated/angry/ unhappy right now, but I can't respond to you when you're behaving like this. Let's talk about this again when you've cooled down.*

In this chapter I offer a few suggestions you can use when you're responding to a case of bad attitude.

Try not to react immediately. Often our first impulse when dealing with snarky is to deliver snarky right back. This is a wonderful opportunity for you to practise the pause. Moments like these give you the chance to remember that you are the adult. Fighting fire with fire might feel good for a moment, but in the long run you're much better to remain calm. Pause before you react.

Find methods of staying calm that work for you. You have an incredible opportunity in this moment to model a calming strategy. Try saying something like: *I'm feeling really angry right now. I think we both need time out, and we can discuss it again once we've both calmed down.* This is an effective technique for diffusing a potential blow-up. Remember, kids often copy what they see. When you struggle with your reactions, don't be surprised if your daughter follows suit.

Use these outbursts as teachable moments. Once your daughter has calmed down and the dust has settled, complete one of the activities in the book that are designed to promote reflection. We all play a role in maintaining peace and harmony within our homes. Let's not raise victims of circumstance; rather, let's raise girls who have the ability to take responsibility for their actions.

Pick your battles. If we challenged our tween daughters every time they showed us attitude, we would be spending a lot of time criticising them. Sometimes no response is the best response.

Or, rather than reprimand your daughter in that moment, a more appropriate response could be to leave the conversation until a later time.

A good opportunity could be when you're both together in the car. You might say something like: *I've been thinking about what you said the other day. Let's talk about it. What was going on for you when you said that?*

You can often end up having a more effective and honest conversation after the event has passed.

Choosing not to respond can be a real test of your self-control. Sometimes all you need to say is that you're not going to respond to that behaviour. Remember, through your actions you are modelling appropriate strategies. You may not always get it right, but each and every time gives you the opportunity to do it better than the time before.

10

A SPECIAL BOOK

As your daughter grows older, she may become less forthcoming with information about how she is and how she's doing. For instance, 'How was your day?' might be greeted with 'Good'. Responses like that can make it hard for you to encourage her to open up.

Of course, the flip side of this is that your daughter might choose to open up to you when you're knee deep in tasks like preparing dinner, making lunches or answering emails, and your response could make her feel that you don't have time for her.

A powerful way to overcome this is to set up a special 'book' that is just for the two of you. It doesn't have to be anything fancy; an exercise book from the supermarket will suffice. Tell your daughter this book is just for you and her. Let her know that if there's something she wants to share with you, perhaps even something she feels embarrassed to talk about, the book is always there.

This works like the box and notepaper I would keep near the door in my classroom for my students.

The beauty of this way of communicating is that it gives you time. My tween daughter will often come to me and let me know that she has written in our book. When I have a moment where I know I won't be interrupted, I sit in a quiet place and give my full attention to reading and responding to my daughter's thoughts.

We don't use the book all the time—weeks and months can pass without either of us writing in it—but it remains a powerful tool. It is our way of staying connected, and reinforcing that all-important mother-and-daughter bond.

11

BODY IMAGE AND YOUR DAUGHTER

When I was young, my mum battled with her weight. I watched her diet and lose weight, stop dieting and gain weight, binge on snacks, and then go back to dieting again. Without her needing to say anything, I internalised the idea that smaller bodies were better bodies.

I went on my first diet at the age of twelve, unbeknownst to my mum, and continued to fight my body until I came out about my private battle with an eating disorder at the age of forty-two.

I tell you this story because my eldest daughter was six when I first noticed her copying my food habits. She began refusing carbs because that's what I was doing. She stepped on the scales first thing in the morning because that's what I was doing. I was role-modelling this behaviour for her.

Zara B, Age 10

THE TWEEN MOTHER'S TOOL BOOK

The realisation that I was setting her up for a lifetime of struggle and disorder was a slap in the face unlike any other. I knew I had to change my ways, but I had no idea how to accept myself just as I was, and so my journey of undoing began. I unlearned everything I had believed to be true. I challenged all my beliefs about food and my body. I attended therapy. I researched. I read and I questioned, and as I gained new understanding I felt a calling to share what I knew. This led to me writing my first book, 'Mirror Mirror On My Wall: A powerful guide for mothers wanting to reflect health and positive body image for their daughters'.

Body-image issues, and helping mothers become better role models for their daughters, became my passion. If this was my story—and I considered myself a highly educated, strong and capable woman—then I knew it was the story of many others as well, and I had to give it my voice. I knew I was not alone in my struggles.

As a mother, like me you probably want more than anything to protect your daughter from going through some of the hardships you've experienced, especially if those struggles involve body shame and accepting yourself as you are. A great place to start is by helping your daughter focus on what her body can do, which is more important than how her body looks.

The following activity is a great way to get the conversation started, and to remind yourself that your body is incredible. Everyone's body is incredible, even if it doesn't look like everybody else's.

My Body

What my body does for me:

_____

_____

_____

_____

What I love about my body:

_____

_____

_____

_____

Things that are unique about me:

_____

_____

_____

Words that remind me how amazing I am:

_____

_____

_____

_____

12

SELF-BELIEF COMES FROM WITHIN

When young girls enter the tween years—eight to twelve—puberty rears its head and they become much more aware of their bodies, an awareness that is often the start of them becoming self conscious. This can be an incredibly difficult time for them, particularly for early developers, who have bodies that appear foreign to them and draw the attention of others.

This is when we have to help our tween daughters acknowledge the incredible things about them that have absolutely nothing to do with their bodies. I call this 'doing the inside work' because that's where the focus is: on the inside.

When my tween daughter was in grade three, there was a day at the beginning of the year when she came home really flat. Her friendship issues had begun in grade two, with many strong personalities trying to assert themselves, my daughter included. On this particular day she felt defeated because she realised that despite new people in her class, she was in for another year of drama with a handful of even stronger willed girls than the year before.

She had had a rough day. She felt alone, and that no one liked her. I asked her to get a pen and some paper, and we sat down in a quiet room to do the following activity together.

I asked her to write down ten things she liked about herself, and I did the same about myself. When we'd finished, we did it again, but this time we wrote down ten things we liked about each other. When we were done, we read our lists to one another, and then swapped lists. The result was that we each had a physical reminder of twenty things about ourselves that were pretty cool.

I can still remember, all these years later, the look on her face and the way her shoulders lifted as she read the things about her that were special. This activity had reminded her that there were many things about her that were awesome, and now she had a list she could go back to time and time again, whenever she needed a pick-me-up.

I encourage you to take the time to go through the same exercise with your daughter, and I hope you experience the same results.

A word of caution: for some people, it can be difficult to think of positive things about themselves. We live in a world where it can be easier to put ourselves down than to build ourselves up. It's time to break that cycle. It's up to each and every one of us to challenge the voices that say we aren't good enough, and we have to teach our kids early on that self-belief comes from within. If we only listen to what others think about us, there's a good chance we'll never know how truly wonderful we are. Remember, no one else is you, and that is your superpower.

Remind your daughter that she is *allowed* to say positive things about herself. She is *allowed* to think that she is smart and funny and worthy. In fact, it's *important* for her to think those things about herself. Now ask her to list and celebrate all the things that make her what she is.

Things I Love About Being Me

THE TWEEN MOTHER'S TOOL BOOK

13

DEALING WITH COMMENTS ABOUT THE BODY

When you were growing up, did a well-meaning adult ever say something about your body that hurt you? Did you have a friend who made you feel embarrassed about your body? Were you ever body-shamed? If you answered yes to any of these questions, you're not alone.

Going through puberty can be a difficult time for young girls. They gain weight because they are meant to, and they fill out, taking on a more womanly shape. This is also the time they become incredibly aware of their changing bodies, so when Uncle Bob says something about his niece's 'development', the comment can be both humiliating and horrifying to the young girl.

Change rooms at school can also be a place for unsolicited commentary on girls' bodies, with flippant remarks like 'you're fat' or 'look at how your tummy pokes out' burning deep holes into their previously intact self-image.

We need to support our tween daughters through these times.

One of the best things I've ever read was a story about a little girl who was running around the school playground when a boy yelled at her, 'You're fat.' She stopped, turned around and yelled back, 'My body is exactly the way it's meant to be,' before running off and continuing her day. If only we could all embrace that little girl's inner warrior.

Words hurt.

The following activity is a way for your daughter to release the words of others to ease their impact. As females, our bodies are never the problem; it's the way other people view them. We are not ornaments to be commented on. Our bodies are our homes: they need to be cared for and respected, and other people's junk mail is not allowed in. My body is my business. Encourage your daughter to get the words out onto paper and then destroy the piece of paper.

Other People's Comments

Someone said my body is

_____

_____

_____

_____

The words hurt me and made me feel

_____

_____

_____

_____

I need to remember that my body is one small part of me and that it's amazing. I'm made up of my mother and her mother before her and all the women in my family. My body does not need to look like anyone else's to be worthy. I am strong and there's no one else on this earth just like me. I will not let the opinions of others make me feel bad about myself.

- I am amazing.
- I am special and I am worthy.
- I am me.
- I will let go of their words and move on with my head held high.
- I will not let the opinions of others define me.

Isabelle K, Age 10

14

PUBERTY QUESTIONS

As our daughters head toward the onset of puberty, they will undoubtedly have lots of questions swirling around in their heads. Your daughter may be really open and happy to ask you questions, like mine is, or she may be shy and reserved, finding the whole period and body change thing utterly embarrassing and cringeworthy to think about.

Regardless of how they feel about it, puberty is coming!

A great way to support them during this time is to create a trusted space for questions. You could create something called a 'wonder box' where they can let you know all of the things they're wondering about, or you could call it the 'girl chats' or 'puberty chat box'. Whatever you call it is totally up to you. Perhaps you could come up with a name for it together!

Give your daughter some paper and encourage them to write down their wonderings when they have them. Reassure them that no question is a silly one, and that this is a safe space for asking questions and sharing between the two of you.

The beauty of this is that it gives you time to think about your responses, and if ever you're unsure of an answer, you have time to find it. Be open and honest with them, and if you had to look for an answer, tell them. They'll appreciate knowing that you took the time to find out something important for them, and it also role models being ok with not knowing it all!

Some of the most common questions are:

Q: What is puberty?

Put simply, puberty is a normal stage of development where your body changes to become more like the body of an adult.

Q: What's going to happen to my body?

The very first subtle change is that your hands and feet get bigger. You might start feeling clumsy and a little uncoordinated but that will pass. Your body will put on weight, your tummy will soften, your hips will widen, you'll start getting taller, and all of that is completely normal and necessary.

(Mums, if you have your own issues around weight and fear of weight gain, now is the time to address this for yourself. Society has taught you that fat is bad, but you cannot and must not pass on these fears to your daughter. As it is, she too is growing up in a fatphobic society, but puberty weight gain is normal and necessary, and you need to be there if and when someone comments on her changing body.)

Your breasts will bud and they'll feel like little tender lumps on your chest. You might start noticing a bit of white/clear gooey stuff in your undies, called discharge, which is perfectly normal and the way your body prepares for your first period (which usually arrives six to twelve months after this).

You'll start to get some dark, coarse body hair under your arms and in your genital area; maybe even more hair on your arms and legs as well.

The order that all of this happens in is slightly different for everyone, and that's okay too.

Q: What happens when I get my period?

You might get a bit moody because of the changing hormones in your body, and feel some cramps in your tummy. Your first period might be bright red blood, or it could be a reddish-brown colour: both are normal. The first few years of your period may be very irregular, with them happening anywhere from every 21 days up to every 35 days. This will eventually even out to being every 28 days. You will bleed for three to five days, and it will range from heavy, to medium to a light flow.

Q: When will I get my period?

There is no easy answer. Most girls get their periods anywhere between eight and thirteen years of age. Mine began the day before I started Grade 6, two months shy of my eleventh birthday. Some will start early, some later.

Mums, talk to your daughter about when you got your first period. If you got yours really early, she may have a similar experience.

The best sign that your body is getting close to having your first period is the appearance of vaginal discharge, which shows approximately six to twelve months before your first period arrives.

Q: What is the difference between a pad and a tampon?

Simply put, a tampon soaks up the blood from the inside, sort of like a sponge, and a pad catches the flow externally, like a piece of absorbent nappy. I still remember putting a tampon in a glass of water to watch how it worked; probably an idea I read in Dolly Magazine!

Depending how heavy the flow is that you are experiencing, you will change pads every recess and lunchtime while at school. It's not advisable for our younger girls to be wearing tampons unless you've received advice otherwise.

Mums, look into 'period underwear': they aren't cheap, but they will help our daughters avoid those worries that we experienced, where we'd freak out that we'd leaked through our school dresses. Depending on the type of period underwear you purchase, your daughter may be able to go all day without worrying about having to change. I wish we had these when I was growing up!

When my daughter asked me this question, I asked her what she thought was going to happen to her body. It was a good chance to find out what she understood already.

One of the most important things we can do to help our girls is to normalise all the things that will change when their bodies go through puberty.

Your hands and feet will grow

Your body will gain weight around your tummy and hips

You will grow dark, coarse hair under your arms and in your genital area

You may get more hair on your legs and arms

Your breasts will bud

Your skin may get oily

Now is your chance to open up. Were you self-conscious as a child? What do you wish you'd understood back then that you know now? When did you start to feel comfortable in your own skin?

Change/Growing up/Sister relationships

In this picture a young lady is going through puberty and her little sister is looking up to her BIG sister with admiration!

Alexia P. 9 years old

Alexia P., Age 9

Q: When will I need a bra?

As soon as you start noticing your daughter hunching her shoulders in an effort to hide her budding chest, you could suggest going shopping for a sports bra. My 9-year-old daughter wears them, not because she needs one yet, but because it gives her extra confidence when cartwheeling and doing things where her t-shirt may lift.

The best answer to this question is, whenever you want to have a special date to go purchase one.

Q: Will I get pimples?

It's more than likely that at some point you will experience pimples. I've already assured my children that I've got them covered when that time arises.

Mum, talk to your daughter about the importance of skin care and cleanliness. Provide her with her own special stash of products suitable for younger skin so that she can feel a little grown up about taking responsibility for the health of her skin.

I remember I had a friend who tried to cover her pimples with band-aids: they became something we couldn't take our eyes off.

Reassure your daughter that pimples are normal, but if she suffers from an extreme case, please take her to your GP so that she can get on top of it.

Q: When can I shave my legs?

This is often a contentious one. My daughter has always had very hairy arms and legs. Each year, starting from Prep, she's talked about her hair. I've encouraged her to accept herself just as she is, but the older she gets, the more willing I am to have this conversation with her.

If our daughters are very self-conscious because they are hairier than normal, or others are making fun of them, an easier option than just telling them to get used to it, is to help them.

15

CELEBRATING HER FIRST PERIOD

*I*n my household, we have always talked excitedly and positively about what to expect with puberty: the body changes, the weight gain, the periods … you name it, we've had an upbeat discussion about it. Through the work I've done with many mums, I know this isn't always how it goes, and in some families these topics are approached with trepidation.

Your tween daughter may be unwilling to listen. She may find the ideas too much to bear, and that's okay. I always say that taking an empathetic approach is appropriate if your daughter is struggling with what puberty will bring her. After all, once she gets her period she will bleed for five days every month for the next forty years, so what's to get excited about?

I can still remember the day I got my period for the first time. I was home alone, it was the day before I started the sixth grade, and I was getting ready for a day out with my grandmother and her cousins. I was dancing in the mirror when I kicked my leg up high and noticed blood. I spent the rest of that day with what felt like a whole roll of toilet paper in my underwear, sitting on the edge of a chair praying I wouldn't bleed through my skirt.

You may find this hard to believe, but a few years ago when I was on school camp as a teacher, one of our students got her period for the first time, and this poor girl actually thought she was dying. Despite the life-education program she would have sat through at school, no one in her family had talked to her about her period and what to expect.

This time in our daughters' lives needs our attention.

It's important that your daughter knows what to expect, so when she starts to gain some weight and her clothes begin to tighten you can remind her of how exciting it is, and how incredible her body is. This is also an important opportunity to talk about kindness to others and not making comments about other people's bodies; we all develop in our own time. Her tummy will soften and her breasts will begin to bud. Generally the first period comes about twelve months after the budding of the breasts.

You want this time to be really special for your daughter, not a time where she freaks out and feels shame and embarrassment at her changing body. It will help to remember how you felt when you got your period for the first time.

Create a First-Period Box

You can help make your daughter's first bleed a positive experience, starting by preparing a first-period box for her and keeping it at the ready for when hers arrives. Things you can put in the box:

Heat pack/hot-water bottle	Hot-chocolate sachets
Period underwear	Pads
Small purse to hold the pads	Chocolate
Diary and pen for tracking dates	Face wash
Perfume	Voucher for a special day out for the two of you

Extra ideas:

Ella S

16

DEALING WITH BIG EMOTIONS

It's inevitable that you will have battles with your daughter during her tween years. She is finding her place in the world, often pushing boundaries and testing your patience while she's at it. It can be a time of outbursts and irrational behaviour that will leave you feeling like you're losing your mind. One minute you have a lovely, compliant daughter and the next you're dealing with a screaming, demanding, nonsensical girl.

These outbursts and challenging behaviours are completely normal, knowledge that probably won't help you much when you're in the middle of experiencing them.

I think of these outbursts as bad-weather events—storms that take us by surprise, blowing through suddenly and upsetting the harmony and peace we had previously known. Can you stop a storm when it's passing through? No. You can baton down the hatches and hope not too much gets damaged when you're in the midst of it, but there's not a thing you can do to stop it when it's coming your way.

Your daughter's outbursts will be a little like that. When one is happening, any amount of yelling and frustration from you won't prevent it from running its course. If anything, that will probably add to it and make it worse. You need to stay calm and wait for these behavioural events to run their course, and then and only then step in to help pick up the pieces.

The following activity is a little along the lines of the restorative practice used in schools after an incident has occurred. It's a way of helping everyone reflect calmly on their role, and offers them the opportunity to see their own behaviour clearly and come up with ideas for next time.

Use the following activities as discussion prompts, or print them out and get together with your daughter so you can both fill them in as individuals accountable for their actions. How you choose to use them is up to you, but it's important that you do use them.

Restoring order after an outburst clears the air and allows everyone to move forward in a better, more positive way—until the next time.

Owning My Behaviour (for Daughters)

I was really angry before, and I

_____

_____

_____

I wish that instead of acting that way I'd

_____

_____

_____

Next time I'm going to try to

_____

_____

_____

What I need from you when I'm feeling like that is

_____

_____

_____

I promise to try to be the best version of myself that I can be, but I'm human and I'm learning and maturing. I won't always get it right, but I am working on it.

Owning My Behaviour (for Mums)

When you were angry I

_____

_____

_____

That made me feel

_____

_____

_____

I wish I had

_____

_____

_____

Next time I'm going to try to

_____

_____

_____

It's important that you know how much I love you, even when I don't like your behaviour. I make mistakes, too. Sometimes I don't handle your outbursts as well as I could, but I'm trying. Let's keep working through things together.

We don't automatically become people who understand ourselves. Reflecting on, and taking responsibility for our behaviour and our actions is something we need to practise. The following activity will help our daughters understand themselves a little better.

Understanding My Emotions

When I get angry I

and I need you to

When I'm sad I

and I need you to

When I'm moody I

and I need you to

When I'm not feeling good I

and I need you to

Sometimes I need to be alone so I

and I need you to

Sometimes we need to come up with better ways of doing things, and a good way of starting is to build a list of options:

Instead of yelling I could

_____

_____

_____

_____

_____

Instead of slamming doors I could

_____

_____

_____

_____

_____

Instead of name-calling I could

_____

_____

_____

_____

_____

_____

_____

Instead of whinging I could

_____

_____

_____

_____

_____

_____

_____

Instead of fighting I could

_____

_____

_____

_____

_____

_____

17

HELPING WITH CHORES

One of the greatest challenges of the tween years is watching your once helpful daughter become someone who rolls her eyes when she's asked to do things. The strategies outlined in this chapter can support you when it comes to encouraging compliance.

Consistency is key. If you have jobs in your home that family members are responsible for (e.g. emptying the dishwasher, clearing the table after a meal) be consistent with your expectations. If you enforce the rules one day, but feel too tired to deal with the complaints the next day and do things yourself, you're sending the message that with the wrong attitude your daughter can get away with not doing things.

Keep in mind that your daughter is trying to assert her independence, and her non-compliance is part of that. Pushing boundaries and seeing how far she can go is a perfectly normal although frustrating stage of her development.

Refer back to your family's essential agreement in chapter 1. What is non-negotiable? Is helping out something that has been agreed on to make the household run successfully? If so, encourage your daughter to just get on with it.

Once you establish the chores in your household, set deadlines. For example, you could say something like: *The dishwasher needs to be emptied within the next half an hour.* It will feel like a request, rather than a demand to empty the dishwater right then and there. Offering a deadline means your daughter will feel she has a level of control. Back off and avoid becoming a micromanager.

Your daughter might want to know what's in it for her. You have to help her understand that everyone has to do what's necessary to get the things they want. If she wants screen time, first she has to do her jobs. Keep it simple. Not everything in life can be fun, and things still have to get done. This is an important message to teach your daughter.

Instead of feeling like you're constantly nagging your tween daughter to do things, use one word. For example, 'bathroom' lets her know that the bathroom needs cleaning; 'bins' will remind her that the rubbish needs taking out. You could work together at a family meeting to come up with appropriate consequences for not doing jobs.

Be predictable rather than angry. If your daughter hasn't done her job, anger and frustration aren't going to help. Instead, go back to your agreed-upon repercussions of not following through with your family's expectations. Consistency is key.

Don't worry about upsetting your daughter. If she isn't angry with you some of the time, you're not doing things right. Your job is not to make your daughter like you. Stay consistent, shrug off the eye rolls, don't bite, and stay on message.

Be honest with yourself about how you were at her age. I remember very clearly shoving all my clothes under my bed, or stuffing as much as I could inside my cupboard in hopes that my mum wouldn't open it. We weren't born as women who love cleanliness, structure and order, so keep that in mind. Your daughter is normal and you will get through this.

Samantha V, Age 12

18

CREATING A DEEPER UNDERSTANDING

When you think back to yourself at your daughter's age, there may be things you wish your own mum had known about you that could have improved your relationship and the way you communicated with each other. Although it's not possible to change your past, together you and your tween daughter can change your future.

You could start by letting her know a few of the things you wish you had known when you were growing up. A few suggestions:

- It's okay to be yourself.
- You're good enough just as you are.

- There's no wrong way to have a body.
- We're all perfectly imperfect.
- It's cool to be smart.
- You don't own your friends.
- It's okay to be different.
- Your looks are the least interesting thing about you.
- Not everyone has to like you.
- There will always be someone prettier, faster or smarter, and that's okay.
- Another person's beauty or success doesn't take away yours.
- Health doesn't have a size.
- All bodies are worthy.
- Our society profits from women's insecurities.
- Diets don't work, they never have and they never will.
- Loving yourself just as you are is a gift.

This next activity is for your daughter to complete. Here is her opportunity to give you the information you need in order to become who she needs. This is a chance for her to open up and for you to understand her a little better. The list should be about the way your daughter feels about certain things, including her thoughts, fears and hopes. It's important you make it clear that everything she tells you will stay between the two of you.

Things I Want You to Know

Dear Mum,

Here are some things I want you to know:

_____

_____

_____

_____

_____

_____

_____

_____

_____

_____

_____

_____

_____

_____

_____

_____

Holly W, Age 8

19

SIMILARITIES AND DIFFERENCES

Both my daughters love private chats. They love the opportunity to have one-on-one time with me, where we can connect and tell stories, and each girl can ask questions and have me all to themselves.

The following activity can be used in a few ways. You could fill this in yourself and put it away for your tween daughter to read at another time. Or you could work through the sheet together, almost as though you were making a time capsule of this period in your lives that she could share with her own children when they're her age. Or you could use the items as prompts to create discussions when you're in the car together, walking around the shops, or baking a cake together.

However you decide to approach it, it's a great way to connect. My tween daughter still can't believe that telephones used to be attached to walls and that I grew up without the internet.

When I Was Your Age

When I was your age, my favourite thing to do was

_____

Your favourite thing to do is

_____

When I was your age, I wanted to be a

_____

You want to be a

_____

When I was your age my friends were

_____

Your friends are

_____

When I was your age, I felt like I was

_____

You feel like you are

_____

When I was your age, I didn't like

You don't like

When I was your age my parents were

That used to make me feel

I wanted to become a mum because

I wish my parents had told me

I want you to know

I love you.

THE TWEEN MOTHER'S TOOL BOOK

20

THE POWER
OF 'YET'

Psychologist Carol Dweck coined the phrase 'the power of yet' in her book, *Mindset*. Our mindset and the way we view situations can mean the difference between sinking and swimming in life. We can be victims or we can be survivors. We can be getting closer or we can be flailing. We can be glass-half-full or glass-half-empty thinkers. The approach we take, and the mindset we have when we enter situations, matters.

When we change our self-talk from 'I can't' to 'I can't *yet*', a weight is lifted and suddenly life feels much easier to manage.

Your tween daughter will not just pick this up on her own, unless by good fortune she's an innately positive thinker. Most mums will need to coach their daughters towards a more optimistic mindset as these young girls take on the challenges and struggles of doing hard things.

Perhaps this is an area you need to work on, too. If so, now is your chance to model the use of 'yet' in your sentences when you talk about new things that you're taking on that you haven't had success with yet.

This is a fantastic way for your daughter to prove to herself that she can do hard things in her own time, with effort and persistence—without your interference but with your support.

It will require some patience at your end. There may be times when you feel like you're banging your head against a brick wall as she fights your 'yet' with her negativity, but don't waver. Calmly reinforce the 'yet' and your faith in her ability to achieve her desired outcome.

If you think of a challenge as exercising a muscle, it will remind you of why it's so important to let your daughter do hard things on her own. Your daughter can record the things she thought she couldn't do, but did. It's important for her to celebrate her achievements and be proud of herself.

My Yet List

What I can't do yet	Date	Date I did it	How I felt when I did it	Steps I took to get there

The Hard Things I've Overcome

THE TWEEN MOTHER'S TOOL BOOK

21

BONDING

ind a time when your tween daughter and you are alone, and have a bit of fun asking each other these questions. Make it a special time for you both by adding background music, food treats and drinks, and finding something online to laugh at before you begin.

- What would you rather have, hands instead of feet, or feet instead of hands?
- Would you rather hold a snake or a spider?
- Would you rather have two close friends or lots of acquaintances?
- Would you rather eat a dead bug or a live worm?
- Would you rather set the table before dinner or clean up after dinner?
- Would you rather lie to your parents or lie to your best friend?
- Would you rather give up technology for a month or not eat treats for a month?
- Would you rather be very short or very tall?

- Would you rather be invisible or be able to read minds?
- Would you rather be the best player on the losing team or the worst player on the winning team?
- Would you rather be a doctor or a scientist?
- Would you rather be very strong or a really fast runner?
- Would you rather lose your sense of taste or your sense of smell?
- Would you rather forget who you are or not know who everyone else is?
- Would you rather be the smartest person alive or the funniest person alive?
- Would you rather be five years older or five years younger?
- Would you rather live without music or without movies?

You could also start a mother-and-daughter wish list. You'll find it helpful to build a list of things you would both like to do together. It could be having a picnic, taking a walk along the beach, visiting a gallery, going shopping, or baking together.

Our Wish List

Things we like to do together:

_____

_____

_____

_____

_____

_____

Things we want to do together in the future:

_____

_____

_____

_____

_____

_____

_____

A LOVE LETTER

Some days are harder than others. We all know this, because we all struggle; struggle is part of life, and is normal and necessary. The following activity is a beautiful one because it allows you to do something special for your tween daughter when she's having a day where she is down on herself. Leaving this on her pillow to find is such a lovely way to let her know that you care, that you're there for her, and that she is special, even on the days she believes it's not true. If your daughter is anything like mine, this note from you will be cherished.

What I Love About You

Dear _____

When you're having a hard day, or if you're feeling down, I want you to look at this list and remember how special you are and how much you are loved.

I love

_____

_____

_____

_____

I love

_____

_____

_____

_____

_____

I love

_____

_____

_____

_____

_____

THE TWEEN MOTHER'S TOOL BOOK

I love

_____

_____

_____

_____

I love

_____

_____

_____

_____

I love

_____

_____

_____

_____

I love

_____

_____

_____

_____

Tori B, Age 11

COMMUNICATION

One of the things I still remember about being a young person is the deflation and frustration I felt when I wanted to talk to my mum about something, only to have her try to fix the situation with her opinion, or give me all the reasons why I was wrong. It wasn't until my early adulthood that I finally addressed this issue with her. As a result, I made a mental note to be a listener first with my own children, although in reality I sometimes still get this wrong.

These days, I ask my tween daughter when she wants me to talk and when she wants me to listen. If she says listen, that's exactly what I do. I don't interrupt and I don't make comments; I lead with my ears. When she has finished speaking, I ask her if she wants my thoughts, or if she just wanted to get it off her chest. More often than not she wants to hear what I have to say.

There's something powerful in the way you communicate with others when you're respectful of their needs.

There will be times when your daughter just wants you to listen, and other times when she wants your advice. It will make things easier for both of you if you know what she needs. These communication passes are a fun way for her to let you know exactly that. All she has to do is circle the appropriate words. She can make a whole bunch of them and keep them ready for when she needs to use them. Give it a try.

Communication Pass

Mum I need to talk to you. I want you to listen/give me advice.

Mum I need to talk to you. I want you to listen/give me advice.

Mum I need to talk to you. I want you to listen/give me advice.

Mum I need to talk to you. I want you to listen/give me advice.

Mum I need to talk to you. I want you to listen/give me advice.

Mum I need to talk to you. I want you to listen/give me advice.

Mum I need to talk to you. I want you to listen/give me advice.

THE TWEEN MOTHER'S TOOL BOOK

SWITCHING THE NEGATIVE TO THE POSITIVE

*T*here is no denying that humans are pretty complex beings. We worry about the future, feel scared of the unknown, and are generally biased more toward the negative than the positive.

Many of us fall into this trap of focusing on the unfavourable. For example, we might hear from nine people that we've done an amazing job of something, but if one person makes a negative comment, we focus on that instead. Why is that? The answer has to do with our evolution.

The term most often used is 'negative bias'. Research shows that our brains evolved to react more strongly to negative rather than positive experiences. For one thing, it kept us safe from danger. So how do we help shift ourselves away from this natural bias?

Research shows that practising gratitude is a powerful way of shifting our focus onto what we have rather than what we don't have. If you physically write down any positives you can think of on a regular basis—so much so that it becomes a habit—you will gradually gain the ability to retrain your brain.

Once you know that you're wired toward the negative you can become more aware of the bias, and when you recognise it you can then try to challenge your thinking on it.

There are so many wonderful gratitude prompts out there. I'm a huge fan of The Resilience Project and their use of the acronym GEM, which stands for *gratitude, empathy, mindfulness*. Their suggested gratitude questions:

- What were three things that went well for you today?
- Who is someone you feel really grateful for today? Why?
- What is something you're looking forward to tomorrow?

(The Resilience Project: www.theresilienceproject.com.au/at-home/learning/gratitude)

I use these prompts in my home to aid dinner-table conversations. They're a great way for us all to connect with one another and move the focus towards a more positive outlook.

Another wonderful activity for releasing negativity is to put your worries down on paper. Starting a 'release' journal is an amazing way to move things from inside of you to outside of you. It's an acknowledgement and a release all at once. Once you've written your worries down, you've released some of their power. Sometimes it can be helpful to sleep with a pen and paper by your bed, so if a worry bothers you during the night, you can get it out of your head and onto paper.

My Release Journal

I'm worried about

_____

_____

I'm worried about

_____

_____

I'm worried about

_____

_____

I'm worried about

_____

_____

I'm worried about

_____

_____

I'm worried about

_____

_____

I'm worried about

_____

_____

I'm worried about

_____

_____

25

DEALING WITH SELF-DOUBT

The tween years are undeniably full of ups and downs, and as much as we try to build up our daughters, they will inevitably have times where they don't feel good about themselves. There will be times when your daughter is filled with self-doubt. Perhaps a friend made a comment on her work at school, or maybe someone flippantly told her she was no good at something she prides herself in.

To support your daughter, help her come up with a list of positive things about herself that make her who she is. A few possibilities:

- I am a good listener.
- I am funny.
- I am caring when people are hurt.
- I am creative.

Creating this list will promote good feelings in your daughter, and the beauty of it is that she will come up with all the pieces herself that make the exercise magical. She should treat the list as a work in progress and remember that it's never finished.

When she's made a good start on the list, have her decorate a jar or box that will become her special container to fill with her 'I am' statements. When she's feeling down, or just needs a reminder that she's more important than others' opinions of her, she could have a lucky dip and find something about herself that's special. Sometimes we could all do with reminders like this.

Ellie K, Age 11

Create an "I Am" Jar

I am

_____

I am

_____

I am

_____

I am

_____

I am

_____

I am

_____

I am

_____

I am

_____

26

SPENDING TIME
TOGETHER

*L*ife can get busy. Even within families, where we all spend so much time in each other's presence, we often lack quality interaction with one another. These coupons are a way for you and your tween daughter to request some special one-on-one time with each other, a way of saying that you miss each other and would like to reconnect. I hope you have fun planning some lovely moments together.

Request Coupons

Dear Mum

I'd really like some extra time with you.

Love

Dear Mum

I'd really like some extra time with you.

Love

Dear Mum

I'd really like some extra time with you.

Love

Dear Mum

I'd really like some extra time with you.

Love

Dear Mum

I'd really like some extra time with you.

Love

Dear _____

I'd really like to spend some extra time with you.

Love Mum

Dear _____

I'd really like to spend some extra time with you.

Love Mum

Dear _____

I'd really like to spend some extra time with you.

Love Mum

THE TWEEN MOTHER'S TOOL BOOK

With the following activity, you both circle one item from each row and then compare your lists.

Things I'd Like to Do With You (for Mums)

Watch a movie at home	Go to the movies
Go for a hike	Walk along the beach
Listen to music	Dance around the house
Do some painting	Do some yoga
Bake a cake	Go to the bakery
Get our nails done	Go to the pool
Play outside	Do some gardening
Play a board game	Read together
Do each other's nails	Do each other's hair
Go for a bike ride	Go for a walk
Get an ice cream	Get fish and chips
Draw together	Write a story together
Look at old photos	Do some crafting
Do a puzzle	Learn something new
Look at baby pictures	Have a dance-off
Learn a new recipe	Have a picnic
Dress each other up	Write a poem about each other
Ask each other questions	Do a photo shoot
Do a meditation	Have a massage
Do a random act of kindness	Write letters

Things I'd Like to Do With You (for Daughters)

Watch a movie at home	Go to the movies
Go for a hike	Walk along the beach
Listen to music	Dance around the house
Do some painting	Do some yoga
Bake a cake	Go to the bakery
Get our nails done	Go to the pool
Play outside	Do some gardening
Play a board game	Read together
Do each other's nails	Do each other's hair
Go for a bike ride	Go for a walk
Get an ice cream	Get fish and chips
Draw together	Write a story together
Look at old photos	Do some crafting
Do a puzzle	Learn something new
Look at baby pictures	Have a dance-off
Learn a new recipe	Have a picnic
Dress each other up	Write a poem about each other
Ask each other questions	Do a photo shoot
Do a meditation	Have a massage
Do a random act of kindness	Write letters

THE TWEEN MOTHER'S TOOL BOOK

27

FRIENDSHIP AND ASSERTIVENESS

When I was young, I had a friend who I rode with on the tram, to and from school. I still remember the day she told me that we could be friends before and after school, but that during school we had to go our own ways. As a young unempowered person, I accepted this. This girl, who was popular and likeable, was someone I wanted to be friends with, and I accepted that our relationship was part-time only. I share this story often in my workshops.

Back then I had no idea that I had the right to better treatment. As adults, if someone treats us poorly, talks behind our backs, makes fun of us or puts us down, we are much more likely to cut them out because, ideally, we have boundaries and know this type of behaviour crosses them. We know that no one has the right to treat us poorly.

Making true friendships at school can be easy for some kids and fraught with challenges for others. Just because you were born in the same year and share the same postcode as someone else, it doesn't automatically follow that you have found your tribe of people. Unfortunately, life doesn't always work like that.

For this reason, it's important to provide your tween daughter with opportunities to create strong friendships outside of school. It can be through sporting activities or any other outside interest. Your daughter needs to learn that she has the right to fair treatment, and you can actively help her in this and empower her to stand up for herself. Children don't have a proper grasp of friendship boundaries until we empower them. You need to let your daughter know that it's okay to have boundaries and that poor treatment crosses the line.

This simple, powerful statement reinforces that concept: *When you make fun of me it really hurts my feelings, and if you keep doing it we can't be friends.*

You may find that your daughter's experiences bring back old feelings connected with your own time at school. As a mum, you feel heartbroken when she suffers, and possibly unresolved anger at the mean girls you endured yourself as your own undealt-with emotions rise to the surface.

Your daughter will take her lead from you, and you need to work with her to become more assertive. If you become angry, she will feel worse; however, if you normalise the situation and take a calm approach, even if you're boiling over on the inside, you will set up your daughter to find more balanced coping strategies.

Self-awareness needs to kick in here, particularly your own. If you're fuming over what's happening with your daughter, check in with yourself to see if there are unresolved issues going on for you. It's important that you don't overreact. Friendship issues, as difficult as they are, are completely normal for young people, and offer opportunities to develop inner strength and resilience.

The following activity addresses some of the most common friendship challenges your daughter will face. By listing the circumstances that require her to become more assertive, she will be able to gauge whether she understands the difference between real and fake friends. It can open the door to some powerful and important conversations around dealing with challenging friendships.

Charlie B, Age 9

Times When I Need to Be More Assertive

Examples:

When I'm excluded from an activity

When my friend makes fun of me

THE TWEEN MOTHER'S TOOL BOOK

28

SUPPORTING POSITIVE FRIENDSHIPS

*I*t's important that we help our tween daughters understand that there are many different types of friends. By talking with your daughter often about what's important in a friend, you can support her as she navigates the ins and outs of friendship as a tween.

So, how can you encourage her to make healthy friendships? You can start by talking with her often about what makes a good friend, and also about how she can be a good friend to someone else. Help her understand that sometimes friendships take work.

With hormones swirling, there will not only be moodiness from your tween, but also among her friends as well. This is a good time for your daughter to learn how to practise the pause. If she doesn't understand her friends' behaviour, encourage her to think what might be going on with them to account for the way they are acting. You can also help her develop meaningful relationships by occasionally including her friends in your family activities.

Teach her the importance of appropriate communication, and make sure she understands that texting isn't an overly effective means of doing this. Explain the importance of body language. Does she smile and make eye contact, or does she avoid it? Is she respectful when others give their opinions, or does she always like to be right? Is she approachable?

Knowing ourselves, and having an awareness of how we come across to others, is important information, but it's just that, information.

Help your daughter choose activities she enjoys, which will provide opportunities for her to form friendships with like-minded others. This is also a good opportunity for you to encourage inclusivity. Being in a clique might look good on the shows she watches, but she will be much better off in the long run if she is someone who is kind to everyone.

If your daughter finds herself in a toxic friendship, empower her to find other friends who will accept her just as she is, and who will make her feel good about herself.

Remind her that friends don't always have to agree. It can sometimes seem easier to just go along with what everyone else is saying or doing, but explain that there is something powerful about asserting yourself and staying true to yourself. She shouldn't be mean to someone just because that's what others are doing. She should know the difference between right and wrong. And be brave.

In this activity, your daughter can list all the attributes she most values in a friend, either a friend she already has or a friend she would like to have.

Things I Value Most in a Friend

_____

_____

_____

_____

_____

_____

_____

_____

_____

_____

_____

_____

_____

_____

_____

There are times when we all feel like there's something wrong with us, but it can simply be that we have a friendship that's not working out. In this next activity, ask your daughter to read through the lists below with her existing friends in mind. If she finds herself ticking too many items in the right-hand column, it may be time to assess the relationship.

Real Friendships Versus Toxic Friendships

Real Friendships	Toxic Friendships
Accept me as I am	Make me feel unsafe
Treat me the same regardless of who else is around	Make me feel stupid
Make me feel good about myself	Use me as the butt of jokes
Are kind	Make fun of me
Support me	Laugh at my expense
Have my back and stick up for me	Spread rumours about me
Make it safe for me to be who I am	Make me feel like I'm not good enough
Celebrate my wins	Make me feel lonely
Encourage me	Don't take an interest in me

29

NEGOTIATING FRIENDSHIPS

*I*f your tween daughter has come to the realisation that a friendship isn't a healthy one, she will need your support to move forward. Friendship boundaries come into play here. A few helpful statements: *It makes me feel unimportant if you roll your eyes when I speak. If you keep doing things like that to me we can't be friends any longer. That's not what real friends do to one another.*

If your daughter uses these statements or similar, she is putting the ball in the other person's court. They will either make improvements, or continue to treat her poorly, in which case she's better off without them.

Breaking up a toxic friendship can be hard. There may be other friends who will side with the other person, but your daughter needs to know that that's okay. She needs to let mutual friends know that she doesn't expect them to choose, but that she has to do what's right for her.

Avoiding getting into a messy break-up is important. Her best tactic is to stay kind, walk with her head held high, and understand that not all friendships last the journey. If things become rough for her at school, encourage her to seek the support of a trusted teacher.

Talk to your daughter about the friendships you've made later in life and reassure her that she has lots of friends out there that she hasn't even crossed paths with yet.

Following is a list of ten possible friendship scenarios commonly faced by young girls. Read through them together, and discuss with your daughter what she could do in each situation. (A cheat sheet follows this list, which you can use as a guide to discussing each scenario after your daughter has answered the questions.)

Friendship Scenarios

1. You're in a friendship group of three, and the other two girls always want to have private chats that don't include you. How do you handle this?

2. You have a friend who is really nice to you sometimes but ignores you at other times. What do you do?

3. One of your friends tells you that another of your friends has been talking badly about you behind your back. How do you handle this?

4. You find out that one of your friends had a party and you were the only one who wasn't invited. What do you do?

5. Your group of friends is always running away from you. How do you deal with this?

6. One of your friends tells you to ignore one of your other friends because of something that happened at recess. How do you respond?

_____

_____

7. You notice one of your friends, the leader of the group, being mean to one of the other girls. What do you do?

_____

_____

8. You always play with the same people at school, but you feel like you want to start playing with others. How do you go about doing this?

_____

_____

9. You hear an unkind rumour about one of your friends. Do you tell them about it? Why/why not?

_____

_____

10. You're constantly being excluded at recess and no one wants to work with you in class. What do you do?

_____

_____

Friendship Scenarios Cheat Sheet

1. Help your daughter understand that no one owns anyone else in a friendship. People are allowed to be friends with whomever they like, and can choose who they want to play with. Empower her to tell her friends that it makes her feel left out when the two of them go off without her.

   - If being the third wheel is a common occurrence for your daughter, support her in finding back-up friends. Ask her if there's anyone else she could become friends with when she has no one to hang around with. Offer playdates and opportunities to extend her social circle.

   - Talk to her about how threesomes in friendships can be challenging. Maybe recall an experience you had when you were her age and tell her how you coped.

   - Listen to her answers; they will tell you a lot about how she manages challenges.

2. Talk about the difference between real friends and sometimes friends. Real friends are not deliberately mean, don't exclude you, and don't make you feel bad. Real friends treat you the same way no matter who is around.

   - This is a great opportunity for discussion. If you had a friend who didn't treat you well when you were growing up, share your experiences with your daughter.

3. Ask your daughter whether she thinks her friend did the right thing by telling you. How does it make her feel to know that someone is saying bad things about her? Discuss the notion that what others think of us is none of our business.

- Talk about whether what others think of us is fact or opinion. What happens when we believe what others say about us more than what we believe about ourselves? Now is your chance to talk about the huge role self-acceptance plays in her life. Explain that she needs to know at a deep level who she is so she can protect herself from hurtful opinions.

- Tell her that although we can never control what others say about us, we can always control how we respond. Does she think her friend did the right thing in telling her, or was that friend just adding to the drama? This question should trigger an interesting discussion.

4. Tell your daughter you understand what a painful experience this can be. If you have a personal story to share, now is a great time to tell it. Ask her why she thinks her friend did this. This is an opportunity to think about what drives someone to be unkind, what their motives are, and what their ultimate intentions are. Sometimes friendships are about control, but does that apply to *real* friendships? What was gained by leaving one person out? What are the ramifications socially?

5. The first thing is to address the immaturity of actions like these. Then ask your daughter how it makes her feel. Why does she think friends would do this to another friend?

   - Being assertive in this situation could involve making statements like this: *When you guys run away from me it makes me feel really sad/lonely/mad. If you keep doing that to me, then we aren't friends.* By making these statements, your daughter is asserting her boundaries and telling others that no one has the right to make her feel unwanted, and if they keep acting in this way she will find people who do want her around.

- This is an opportunity to remind your daughter that not everyone is going to like her, and that's okay. Tell her that she might not be everyone's cup of tea because not everyone has great taste.

6. Here is a chance to discuss intentions. Why does your daughter think her friends would ask her to ignore the other person? What do they gain from this? How does she think it makes the ignored person feel?

- A great way to be assertive in this situation is to say: *I don't think ignoring her is a good idea. If you're upset with her you should talk to her and tell her how you're feeling. Ignoring her is mean and it doesn't solve anything. I don't want to be involved with any of that.*

- Empowering your daughter to do the right thing is so important. She might find herself in a situation that makes her feel uncomfortable, but if she does not know how to make a stand, she may go along with what's happening to make the 'queen' friend happy.

- There are many opportunities here to discuss kindness and the importance of not being a bystander to mean behaviour. When we *know* better, we can *be* better.

7. This calls for a similar response to the assertive responses above. It's likely there will be others in the group who are also feeling disempowered and not speaking up, especially where the 'queen' friend is involved. Helpful comments in this situation could be: *Jessica, I think you need to stop being mean to Cassie. She hasn't done*

anything wrong and what you're doing is really unkind. Can we all just get along?

- Alternatively, if your daughter feels that this is too confrontational, another way of standing up for the person being treated poorly could be to say: *That's really mean. Come on, Cassie, let's go and play somewhere else. You don't deserve to be treated like that.*
- Whichever approach resonates with your daughter, both are empowering. Often people stay quiet out of fear, but what is that fear really about? There's a great chance to unpack that here.

8. Branching out from a friendship group can be scary and exciting at the same time. Your daughter may have friends who take this as rejection. They may take it that she thinks they're not good enough for her, or that she thinks she's better than them. Regardless, if she feels pulled to connect with other people then she should do it.

   - If her friends are feeling angry with her, she could say something like: *I love spending time with you and you're still really important to me. It's just that I'd like to spend some time getting to know other people as well.*
   - Remind your daughter that none of us owns our friends, and it's okay to want to make new friends or play with other people. This can be particularly challenging during the tween years, but if our daughters work through the hard part there are wonderful opportunities on the other side to connect with others.

9. Ask your daughter what she has to gain by telling her friend. Will the friend be hurt? Will it cause drama? Would she be better to address the rumours herself and defend her friend by saying something like: *You need to stop talking like that about Lisa. What*

you're saying is really hurtful and mean. How would you feel if someone spoke that way about you?

- Discuss the pros and cons of her going to her friend with the rumours.

10. The key word here is *constant*. You want to help your daughter differentiate between mean-girl behaviour and bullying. *Constant* means relentless, day in, day out, ongoing exclusion. If your daughter is experiencing this, encourage her to seek support from her teacher. Encourage her to write a letter if she feels uncomfortable speaking to her teacher about it, but do encourage her to act. Teachers can't address what they're unaware of.

- You could also use this opportunity to unpack what it is she likes about these girls that she continues to go back to. How do they make her feel? Use the analogy about a moth to a flame, which is drawn to the light but ends up worse off.

- If this discussion with your daughter brings up bad feelings and sadness, follow it up with a feel-good activity that reminds her that she is an incredible person, whether others see it or not. Talk to her about how sometimes we don't find our tribe until we leave school. Encourage activities outside of school. Help her find a passion. Provide opportunities for her to find other like-minded kids she can form friendships with outside of school, whether that be through a sporting or other group.

30

SAY IT AND GO

nother powerful strategy for developing assertiveness is the say-it-and-go approach. It's powerful because it avoids confrontation and a possible war of words. Tell your daughter that if someone says something that isn't nice, whether to her or a friend, she could say her piece and then walk away. She could make a simple statement like: *That's really rude.*

This approach will make her feel that she has asserted herself, and it takes away the opportunity for the other person to say something back that leads to an argument that could unfold something like this:

That's really rude.

Yeah? Well, I don't care what you think.

Well, you should.

Why should I care about you? You think you're so good.

And on it goes from there. With the say-it-and-go approach you literally do just that. You say your piece and then leave the scene. There are no comebacks, there's no opportunity for defensiveness from the other person; you make a simple statement and walk away.

It's important to point out here that you're not telling the other person they are rude; you're pointing out that what they *said* is rude. There's an important distinction there.

If your daughter were to stand up for a friend, she would apply the same technique but take her friend with her. She could say something like: *That's so mean. Come on, Maddie, let's go.*

31

DEALING WITH WORRIES

We need to teach our tween daughters that worrying about things is normal; we all do it. The difference between it becoming a problem or not is in the way we process our worries. Our thoughts lead to our feelings, which lead to our actions. We need to teach our daughters to tune into their thoughts. When they are feeling anxious about things, what are they saying to themselves?

Common examples of negative self-talk include: *I can't do this. I'm no good. Everyone hates me. I'm so bad at everything. Everyone will laugh at me. I suck.* It's easy to see how having these words swirling around in your head would make you feel pretty terrible about yourself, and thoughts like these can often become quite debilitating.

It's our job to help our daughters unpack this.

Eva I, Age 10

THE TWEEN MOTHER'S TOOL BOOK

Help your daughter understand that the little voice in her head is *hers*. When she feels bad, it's because of what she's saying to herself. She is not her thoughts, she is just the person paying attention to them. And although it might take time, effort and practice, she has the power to control those thoughts and any negative self-talk.

The following list will give your daughter opportunities to pay attention to her self-talk. It is designed to help her work through her anxious thoughts and create more balanced ways of thinking.

Reframing Negative Self-talk

Negative Self-talk	Positive Self-talk
I can't do this.	I can't do this yet.
I'm no good.	Not everyone can be good at everything, and that's okay.
Everyone hates me.	Just because someone doesn't see my worth, it doesn't mean I'm not worthy.
Everyone will laugh at me.	No one is perfect. I'd rather be someone who tries than someone held back by fear.

There is always another perspective if we give ourselves the chance to see it.

Challenging My Thinking

My anxious thoughts	What is actually going on
I'm such a failure.	My mistake doesn't make me a failure; it just makes me imperfect like everyone else.

What if	What is actually likely
I try really hard and I still fail.	You might be disappointed, but you'll also be really proud of your effort.
Everyone laughs at me.	What if they don't? People might be really supportive and kind.

32

SIBLING HARMONY

*D*o your kids fight? Do they nit-pick? Do they have the ability to drive each other totally crazy with a look? Mine do too. As a parent, the sibling relationship can either fill your heart with joy or frustration. In this chapter I offer a few tips to encourage healthy sibling relationships.

It helps to recognise that sibling rivalry is a normal part of growing up. After all, your kids would probably not choose to hang out with each other 24/7; they've been thrown together by the chance of life.

You'll find it easier to cope when your expectation is that this rivalry will continue for a long time, so it pays to get used to the snarky comments: *He's looking at me. She touched my arm.*

Give your kids more of you. This isn't meant to sound tough—I know that as a parent you're probably already being pulled in multiple directions—but often sibling rivalry is all about getting attention. To kids, even negative attention is better than no attention at all. Try to give each of your children ten minutes of uninterrupted time, when they have you to themselves. That means no checking your phone, no screens at all, just your child and your undivided attention. You'll find that this one-on-one time increases your emotional connection.

Sometimes your kids just want to be acknowledged. For example, if one of your children takes something from a sibling, and that child comes to you, your first instinct might be to tell the first child to give it back. What if, instead of responding in that way, you said something along these lines to the aggrieved child: *Did she take your pen without asking? That must be really annoying.* This will validate the child's frustration and make them feel like you've heard them, and they will often go off and deal with it on their own from there.

Avoid pitting your kids against one another. Encouraging a non-sporty child to be more like a sibling who excels at everything, or a creative child to be more academic like a sibling who gets top marks is setting them up for competitive relationships where one comes out on top and the other feels resentful.

Our job as parents is to see our children as unique individuals; it's okay if one is sporty and one isn't. Focus on, and celebrate, their individual strengths. Rather than encouraging one to be as good as or better than another, acknowledge that they are all amazing in their own way.

To take the previous point even further, think about what labelling your children actually does. When you talk about your 'sporty' child, your other children hear that they are not sporty. When you talk about the 'fussy' one, the others naturally assume that they are better.

Rather than unintentionally pitting your kids against one another, praising positive attributes such as kindness, respect and teamwork will stop them competing for your approval.

Be objective and stay calm if you're placed in the middle of a dispute. Refer back to your family's essential agreement in chapter 1. Don't play

Annabelle S, Age 9

favourites, but rather help one child see where the other is coming from. Organise time-outs, and give opportunities to cool down before entering into a discussion about what went on between them.

If one of your children says something to put one of their siblings down, suggest that they find a way to build that other child up again. For example, if one child tells another that they are 'dumb', you could ask the first child to come up with three positive things to say in order to heal the damage of their negative words.

I did this with my own kids when they were little, to great success. I would send the offending child to their room until they came up with three things they loved/respected/liked about their sibling. When the first child looked the other in the eye and said those things, the receiver of the positive words would invariably acknowledge them with a thank-you.

Help your children resolve their conflicts themselves rather than doing it for them. When they're calm, help them to use 'I feel' statements to share their side of the story. Ask them to come up with possible solutions together. If they can't resolve the conflict, you could say something like: *You either work out how you're going to play fairly or the game is going away.* This approach will help them realise it's to their advantage to come up with a solution together.

Make celebrating each other a normal part of life in your home. You could start a celebration box. Put a pen and notepad next to a small box, and encourage family members to write something kind and supportive about someone else. Examples could be: *Well done, Lucy, for helping your brother with his homework this week. Rebecca, thank you for being so kind and sharing your pencils with me.* These notes could be read out on Friday nights as part of a feel-good family activity.

Finally, practise gratitude as a family. This will encourage emotional connection and positive engagement.

33

CONVERSATION STARTERS

The following conversation starters can be used in any way you like. Throw one out if you and your daughter are in the car heading off on a long drive. Cut them up for a weekly dinnertime-conversation lucky dip. There are so many ways you can use them, so get creative and enjoy.

- What would your best day ever look like?
- What is your favourite memory?
- What was the most embarrassing thing that has ever happened to you?
- If you could only eat one food for the rest of your life, what would you choose?
- What is one thing you really want to do?
- What makes a good friend?
- What makes a bad friend?

- How do you know if you can trust someone?
- What is your favourite thing about yourself?
- What would your dream job be?
- If you could only take three things with you on a desert island, what would you choose?
- Do you think it's better to save your money or spend it right away?
- What makes you laugh?
- What's the funniest thing that ever happened to you?
- What's the best thing that happened today?
- Who made you happy today and why?
- Who made you feel cared about today?
- What is something you wish people knew about you?
- What are your three best qualities?
- What are three things about yourself you'd like to work on?
- What does it mean to live a good life?
- Where does your worth come from?
- Is it possible to live a life without telling a lie?
- If you could teach everyone in the world only one thing, what do you think would have the greatest impact?
- What does the phrase 'our struggles make us stronger' mean?
- Why do you think mistakes are important?
- What would be your best advice for someone who is trying to find happiness?
- Why do you think we care so much about what other people think?
- Does what other people think really matter?
- What do you think you'll remember about yourself now, when you're older?
- Are there any original thoughts?
- What would the world be like if everyone looked exactly the same?

THE TWEEN MOTHER'S TOOL BOOK

- What would happen if everyone said what they thought?
- What's a food you really want to try one day?
- What started out badly for you, but ended up being really good?
- When was the last time you were wrong about something?
- If you could have dinner with three people who are dead or alive, who would you choose?
- What's something you're really interested in that others are not interested in?

Conclusion

You have finally reached the end of the book, but perhaps this end is just the beginning. In parting, I'd like to leave you with these beautiful words:

> *If I could give my daughter three things,*
> *They would be the confidence to always know her self-worth,*
> *The strength to chase her dreams,*
> *And the ability to know how truly deeply loved she is.*
>
> —Author unknown

I hope *The Tween Mother's Tool Book* will help you create a connection with your daughter that will last you a lifetime.

Don't forget to come find me online @raisingstrongdaughters_ and at The Mother's Hub Club (www.raisingstrongdaughters.com.au) for ongoing parenting support.

Signing out, from my heart to yours.

Amanda

Printed in Australia
AUHW010831090920
333769AU00001B/1

9 780648 345831